Family Bonding Project

GENERATION
of
ISIS

Where justice is denied, where poverty is enforced, where ignorance prevails, and where one class is made to feel that society is organized in a conspiracy to oppress, rob and degrade them, neither persons nor property will be safe.

Frederick Douglass

GENERATION of ISIS

© 2016, Omar Reda / **Family Bonding Project**
All rights reserved.

No part of this book may be used or reproduced by any means, graphic, electronic, or mechanical, including photocopying, recording, taping or by any information storage retrieval system without the written permission of the author/publisher except in the case of brief quotations embodied in critical articles and reviews.

ISBN: 978-0-9970008-6-3 - *print*
ISBN: 978-0-9970008-7-0 - *ebook*

BOOK DESIGN
timmyroland.com

COVER IMAGE
pixabay.com

THE EFFECTS OF VIOLENCE AND CONFLICT ON CHILDREN

GENERATION
of
ISIS

OMAR REDA MD

Family Bonding Series
volume two

English Version

Family Bonding Project
WORLDWIDE

GENERATION
of
ISIS

Contents

About The Author . . . . *i*
Introduction . . . . *iii*
Background . . . . *v*

What Is ISIS 1
What Does Islam Say About ISIS 3
Youth & Violence 5
Youth & Vulnerability 7
Vulnerability Themes 9
The Stuggles Of Muslim Youth Under ISIS 11
Preventive Measures 13
Interventions 17
Family As the Frontline Defense 21
Predictions 23
Conclusion 25
References 27

GENERATION *of* ISIS

About the Author

Dr. Omar Reda is a board-certified psychiatrist who currently lives with his wife and three daughters in Portland, Oregon.

He graduated from Benghazi Medical School, obtained a Masters certificate in global mental health from Harvard Program in Refugee Trauma, and then finished psychiatric residency at the University of Tennessee.

Dr. Reda chairs the USA section of the Federation for Arab Psychiatrists, the Oregon Muslim Medical Association and heads the Family Bonding Project. He is also actively involved in multiple youth and family healing and empowerment projects nationally and internationally.

Dr. Reda is an expert and a sought-after public speaker on issues of psychological trauma, Muslims' mental health, immigrants' mental health, the Libyan revolution and the Arab Spring.

GENERATION *of* ISIS

Introduction

Unfortunately, violence is becoming the latest human pandemic. The world is growing more dangerous every day with no sign of relief in the foreseeable future.

This writing is by no means a message of pessimism or discouragement, but is rather a realistic look into the root causes and risk factors for youth violence and radicalization, as well as an attempt at paying special attention to ways for prevention and suggested early interventions for this ugly and fatal malignancy.

GENERATION
of
ISIS

Background

I happen to face multiple ugly monsters throughout my life starting from the early tender age of six when I lost my fourteen-year-old sister for brain cancer. She lost her eye sight, and then her health quickly deteriorated despite my parents' frantic attempts to save her life. I fantasized then of becoming a brain surgeon and that ignited my passion for the medical profession. I also remember when I was almost kidnapped at the age of eleven. The man who stopped his car pretending to ask for directions told me to get into the car or else, I ran faster than I have ever thought imaginable and watched him from behind the bushes scanning the area before finally giving up and driving off.

Fast forward, and here I was at age twenty-three working as an emergency physician. I found my passion more in the humanistic rather than the technical aspects of medicine. I loved the field of psychiatry as it was a beautiful mix of art and science. The reason I fell in love with the field was most likely because of the multiple encounters with what I refer to as the invisible elephant, the trauma story.

I remember when I came home from the hospital at age twenty-six to find my father standing at the door, he frantically urged me to flee the country because, for some reason, my name was "placed on the black list of the regime" and that there was a warrant issued for my arrest or assassination.

I ended up in the United Kingdom, living a difficult life of asylum seeking, where people with less than tenth my education and talent looked at me with disgust thinking that I was there to somehow be their competition or steal their "rights".

I came to the USA in 2002, and my journey through the immigration system was another traumatic story, the wounds of September 11th, 2001 were still fresh and bleeding, but why do I need to apologize for a group that I have nothing in common with, and why should me or my family have to pay the heavy price of ignorance, stereotyping and racism.

Things started to improve in 2006 when I got accepted into a global mental health program through Harvard. I learned valuable skills which reignited my passion about trauma therapy and how to best refine my psychosocial skills to help those who deal with the invisible scars of trauma and ugly wars.

In 2011, my home country of Libya went through a bloody revolution that ousted a dictator but not his aftermath. Five years later, Libyans continue to kill one another, and different dark militias and ideologies dominate the already fragile country to arrest the birth of the beautiful child of dignity and freedom. The war also claimed the lives of many loved ones and it continues risking creating yet another group of youth to add to the trans-generational transmission of trauma and dysfunction.

The trauma story was recently brought to my attention in a very powerful narrative that one of my clients shared. She lost her father at an early age and here she was at age eighteen struggling with hearing voices. She was quickly labeled as schizophrenic and was started on powerful medications. When we sat down, I enquired first about the exact nature of the voices and she shared that she was hearing the loud scream of two young girls, I then asked about the death of her father, she said that she only knew as a child that her father died in a car accident, but very recently she learnt that he was driving drunk and had a head-on collision that claimed the lives of two young women.

My patient made it her goal to try to find the families of the victims and apologize on her father's behalf in order for her and them to make some sense out of a non-sense situation, try to make amends, find meaning, forgiveness and closure. What a heavy burden to carry at an early age, and what a disastrous path we could walk the trauma survivors through if we do not treat each other as humans, look people in the eye and listen to their stories.

My most recent and ugliest encounter with the invisible elephant was when my twelve-year-old daughter asked me "dad, what does it mean to see in your nightmare that you are receiving death threats".

I did not know that children that young could put these three scary words "nightmare, death, and threats" in one sentence. We tried our best to shield our girls from the hateful messages instigated in the media, but our children are smarter than what we give them credit for.

I decided to break the silence and face fear and hate head-on, this writing is a modest attempt to stand in the face of a destructive powerful flood, I may die or drown in the process but it is my ethical duty and my children's right to have this work owed and dedicated to their future because they deserve a better world, one that brings them peace, love and healing.

We need to start acknowledging the invisible elephant and work towards healing before it is too late. It is never late to do the right thing.

My multiple encounters with different traumatic memories and the dark side of humanity made me stronger, and I made it my mission to walk proud of who I am, my wounds, story, background, culture, accent and religion. I have nothing to apologize for, and I find it mandatory to share my insights and try to be a sound of reason and a beacon of hope and healing, and not surrender to the many faces of ISIS.

GENERATION *of* ISIS

OMAR REDA MD

What is ISIS

It is no secret that many groups throughout history have claimed to operate under the umbrella of religion in order to obtain short-lived worldly gains.

Violent ideologies had existed since the beginning of time, and they have nothing to do with any religion.

The so called "war on terror" had unfortunately created a very malignant cancer that had spread at a frightening rate since 2001. No one can claim to be safe when it comes to the threat of hate and violence. It does not happen "somewhere else" anymore, the big invisible elephant is making its presence quite known in our very backyards and is shamelessly knocking on our front doors and even our bedrooms.

It is up to every one of us to do our part in eradicating this ugly monster, or else we will all be living under the reign of an angry generation of ISIS.

ISIS I would argue is not only the so called "Islamic State", but a term I would use to describe a phenomenon that has nothing holy or Godly about it.

It is my strong conviction that the so called Islamic State is a group of vulnerable youth turned law-less militias, and a collection of low-life mercenaries who get paid by the "elite" in order to ensure chaos and maintain the status quo.

ISIS cannot be defeated with an attitude of silence, and we cannot fight violence through violence. To carelessly watch and to condone hate is the very goal that this twisted group is trying to achieve.

What does Islam say about ISIS

Islam and ISIS have absolutely nothing in common. On the contrary, it is Islam that orders its followers to save human lives and to spread peace and joy. The Quran teaches us that "if any one killed another, it would be as if he killed the whole of mankind; and if any one saved a life, it would be as if he saved the lives of the whole of humanity".

It is the prophet of Islam Muhammad (PBUH) who told us that the human blood is more sacred than demolishing the house of Allah in Makkah.

The war is not between Islam and the West, the war that should be launched is a fight against all shades of ISIS and all forms of ignorance and misconception, a peaceful war that has weapons of education, compassion, communication and inclusion.

No religion condones violence; God rather condemns sternly all forms of hurting others not only physically but also verbally and emotionally.

God and the authentic divine teachings encourage nothing but safety and security for the whole of humanity.

I happen to thoroughly search the Holy Quran, verse by verse, trying to find any evidence supporting the claim that it promotes violence, or that Islam is inherently evil. What I discovered is that God gave us directions and tools to make our choices in life, and it is up to us to decide how we treat His commands, and then we should not complain facing the consequences of our own actions.

I do not deny the existence of groups that belong to the religion of Islam that use the Quran to justify acts of hatred and violence. They however have much more in common with the enemies of the faith than with its followers, as they both misquote the Quran or take its verses out of context.

Anyone with own agenda can misquote a verse of any scripture, and take a text out of context to seemingly prove a point.

It will do no one justice to keep pointing fingers towards "the other" and fear the unknown, the best cure for ignorance is education, we should rather seek knowledge and actively try to find answers for ambiguous questions and doubtful situations. If we extend a hand and build a bridge then we will be pleasantly surprised that we have much more in common than what we have different, with "the other".

Youth & Violence

Violence causes long-lasting impact on the psyche of its survivors. Children who are forced to be subjected to the ugly weapons of war might struggle with its psychosocial sequelae for generations to come, a heavy price that humanity cannot afford to pay.

War and killing are very ugly concepts even when "necessary", their negative impact stays forever in its witness. Children are more vulnerable as they tend to blame themselves for what happens to others, and because in order for a child to develop a healthy personality they need to believe that the world is a safe place and that adults can be entrusted to protect them.

Children who witness death, rape, intimidation, abuse and torture can struggle with many negative reactions that can be confusing to them and their caregivers, hence the importance of psycho-education.

Adults need to lead by example, so children do not grow up thinking that violence is an acceptable way to resolve conflict.

Post-Traumatic Stress Disorder (PTSD) is a common phenomenon after a traumatic event, which can lead to either the re-experience of trauma through flashbacks and nightmares, the avoidance of reminders of the trauma, or experiencing physical symptoms like shortness of breath, sweating, hand tremors and palpitations. In the case of children, they can have social, behavioral and academic struggles.

My grave concern is for the children who are brainwashed to join the ranks of violent and extremist groups, they face double the trouble, as they go through the abuse by the gang leaders and militant thugs, then they go through the painful experience of taking someone's life, and many cannot see another exit out of that dark tunnel and horrific experience than through continued violence, addiction or suicide.

Youth & Vulnerability

It is no wonder that many children who fall into the traps of violent ideologies are emotionally and psychologically vulnerable, the parasites of ISIS know very well how to prey on victims of opportunity.

Vulnerable youth get drawn or rather sucked into the alluring world of extremism through many different means. With today's technological advances, most of the "recruits" meet their fate online.

The secrecy that cyber spaces provide is very attractive to the darkness-loving shady predators who operate such movements.

Many factors contribute to making youth vulnerable to radicalisation, among those are:

- Dysfunctional family dynamics, Children here fill an emotional void, and get a false sense of belonging that they were not able to obtain from their immediate support circle
- Sense of isolation and marginalization
- Loss of psychosocial support network

- Subjection to the experience of racism and discrimination
- Lack of purpose
- Peer pressure

Warning signs and red flags include:

- Disconnect from family and support system
- Questioning one's identity, faith and sense of meaning and belonging
- Taking interest in violent ideologies
- Change in language and behaviour

There is no one size that fits all though. Those involved in extremism come from all walks of life, and all sorts of backgrounds and experiences. Generally, however, ISIS recruits share one thing in common, vulnerability and desperation.

Vulnerability Themes

- Discomfort in one's own skin (identity crisis)
- Psychosocial issues, for example familial, marital, financial or academic struggles
- Feelings of inability to meet one's full potential
- Legal involvement, like exposure to criminal activities or drugs

Given the global conflict and the many political and humanistic views towards human suffering and violence, it is important to make the distinction between the people who may be emotionally affected (i.e. by the images of death and destruction) and those who are directly sympathetic or supportive of extremist ideologies or acts. People are entitled to their opinion and have the right to support or belong as long as they do not engage in or condone violence.

It is usually the experience of being ignorant, naïve, impoverished, disadvantaged; discriminated against or socially excluded that leads youth to believe in a fantasy, and makes them walk through the valleys of desperation, disillusion, destruction, darkness and death.

Having rigid, black or white, concrete, or skewed views of religion or politics can also be quite dangerous. It is very easy to take a text out of context and paint a whole religion or community with one brush.

It is also important to address the trauma story, hurt people hurt people, wounds that are not nursed, or those left to be open and bleeding might eventually get infected, inflamed or gangrenous.

The Struggles of Muslim Youth Under ISIS

Muslim youth living at the time of ISIS face multiple unfair struggles.

In these difficult times, where Islamophobia is encouraged publically by politicians, fame-seekers and the media, it is a dirty game to try to divide and concur, those who play such games know that the usual losers are the youth who are forced to either question their identity, culture, religion, or feel the need to apologize for who they are, or go into isolation or withdraw, or go to the other extreme, be always on the defensive and easily lash out in offense.

Muslim youth in the west are especially in an extremely difficult position, as their every move is under scrutiny. No child deserves to be under this amount of stress or has to pay for someone else's crime.

What breaks my heart the most is that children living under such circumstances miss out on their childhood and the many opportunities to have healthy interactions with other cultures and religions, we do not need to be a melting pot, we are rather a fruit salad, we are beautiful the way we are, because we are unique, we bring value because we are different, we are an array of colors and flavors that add to the harmonious mosaic.

Preventive Measures

Children who are vulnerable and at risk, need our immediate attention and assistance, not our anger and punishment. We need to get to these children first before they go too far.

In order to stir youth away from delinquent ideologies, either they be racist, ignorant, violent, "terrorist" or other forms of radicalism or extremism, we need to first explore the root causes of the attraction or fascination with such deviated schools of thought and behavior. What are the underlying causes, the driving forces and the missing links that lead young souls away from and completely at odds with their very psychosocial support systems of family, friends and faith.

We cannot fight distorted ideologies with violence, as that will only serve to enforce them. Ignorance is eradicated through education. We need to take those wandering souls into a "time-in" rather than a "time-out" and to have an honest soul-searching journey to nurse their emotional wounds and fulfill their basic needs.

It is through acts of kindness and compassion that bridges of communication and trust get built and wounds start to heal.

To claim that force and punishment is the way to correct misconceptions is an illusion.

Violence and hatred only breed a continuum of strong negative thoughts and feelings if not hostility and bloodshed.

Youth are particularly vulnerable given the difficult times they live in and the daily challenges they face, where the media, misguided or not, adds insult to injury and ignites destructive fires that burn everything and everyone in their way.

Youth need to be sat down with, listened to, talked with, counseled and guided. Every lost soul is a waste of infinite wealth of potential and a shame on all of us.

The way to win the hearts of our youth is to involve and empower them, in other words to make them part of the solution not only part of the problem.

That can be done through comprehensive programs that at minimum should address their safety (physical and emotional), fulfill their basic necessities (of having a voice, freedom, housing, education and decent living), and explore what can the beautiful face behind the mask of pain and dysfunction bring to the table.

Through linking youth with compassionate systems of healthy education and nurture we can face these issues head-on and use early prevention rather than late intervention avenues to lead them back to the path they were created for, to worship God and serve His creation and to make the world a better place.

People "act out" or regress when their sense of safety or identity is threatened or when they feel out of control.

To give them healing spaces that provide a sense of dignity, normalcy and balance, and to provide them with avenues for healthy expression and release of strong emotions, and to challenge their distorted thoughts and channel their behaviors into more productive, cooperative and collaborative than competitive self-centered ways, and to reconnect them with their core beliefs about their own identity, duty towards family, community, society, humanity and spirituality, and to invite and value their ideas, talents, and contribution, is the approach that would prove a worthy investment and one that leaves long-lasting impact on their psyche and allow them to feel empowered and to forgive and be forgiven, make them heal, rehabilitate, reintegrate and be productive members in the rebuilding process.

That, in my opinion, is a much better option than the ugly alternative of pointing fingers, isolation, alienation, blaming and dehumanizing the "other" or going with the motto "you are either with me or against me, either a friend or a foe".

We are rather in this together, we are God's trustees on His earth, we cannot make our world a better place by killing one another, but rather by joining forces and holding hands through the very basic yet universal power of understanding, love, care, kindness and compassion.

LOVE is the only tool that will defeat ISIS, LOVE stands for listening to those crying for help, offering them options, choices, and alternatives, validating their feelings and experiences and empowering them so they try to find their self-worth and achieve their true value and full potential.

Interventions

We need to sit down with these young potential "terrorists" and hear their stories and see things from their point of view.

It is important to voice the message that violence cannot be committed in our name, we need to create a counter-narrative to the story that violent groups are boldly telling.

As the forefront, the family unit must be supported in its effort to challenge misconceptions, provide guidance and offer safe healthy alternatives.

The dialogue of civilizations is an important tool to help youth reject violence; the international community should support such dialogue and promote the positive interactions between cultures, religions and communities.

We need to close the gap between the expectations of an individual and the reality of his or her situation. Hope and faith are too precious to lose, hopelessness breeds desperation, and desperate people do desperate things.

Fighting extremism requires local efforts on a global scale. Small indigenous ways of healing need to be promoted and supported. Think globally and act locally.

Culture and education are the worst enemies of violent extremists, and are our best allies to promote tolerance, inclusiveness and open-mindedness.

Respecting the hopes and aspirations of all sections of the population especially the youth is one of the best antidotes to terrorism.

Government, academia, civil society and the media could play complementary roles, a large scale psychosocial campaign is a vital component in reaching out to potential at-risk youth and families. We need to bring young people back from the frontlines of fighting to the classrooms and playgrounds.

Young people must be provided with a choice, a sense of belonging and a purpose in life.

Some people argue that the first step in addressing youth radicalization is understanding and eradicating conditions conducive to its spread, from underdevelopment to feelings of discrimination.

Marginalization, protracted conflicts, violations of human rights and lack of good governance are possible factors that must be addressed in a holistic approach.

Empowerment of youth and their protection against abuse of modern communication is essential, as is curbing intolerance through alliance, rather than clash, of civilizations.

The future should focus on helping the children wield the tools of peace, justice and development instead of the arms of hatred and terror.

We need to educate children and young people in the values of dialogue and respect for others. Fostering public debate encourages young people to air their frustrations before they succumb to extremist ideologies. Extremist recruiters could be countered through young people themselves as trusted voices, respected among their peers, on the very platforms used to recruit new members.

Accountable institutions and the involvement of especially the youth and women is one of the best ways to contain and rehabilitate "troubled" youth.

Some people suggest a two-track approach in that regard: a hard approach entailing law enforcement measures that punish the wrong-doers, and a soft approach seeking to influence the hearts and minds of people.

Promoting the participation of young people in peace-building requires multiple approaches. These could include:

1. A human rights-based approach
2. An economic approach
3. A political approach
4. A psycho-socio-cultural-spiritual approach

It is important to promote sustainable, long-term and collaborative initiatives for and by young people. Involve hard-to-reach young people and those who belong to groups often disproportionately affected by conflicts, such as disabled young people and young people from marginalized, minority and indigenous groups.

Create opportunities for young people's sustained participation, ownership and leadership in local, national, regional and international mechanisms to prevent, manage and resolve conflict and maintain peace.

Family as the Frontline Defense Against ISIS

I have always been amazed how most of the "issues" we see with children stem from dysfunctional familial and societal dynamics.

I am not trying to discount the biological or genetic etiologies of mental health symptoms, but want to emphasize the interplay of bio-psycho-socio-spiritual factors in the origin and continuation of this symptomatology, and their importance in the healing process.

Children who come from "broken" homes, where parents are either physically or emotionally absent or abusive, or children who are forced to endure the physical, verbal, sexual or psychological sadistic fantasies of adults, or children who are introduced at an early age to the dark and dangerous worlds of drugs and sex, or children who rather use social media to vent their innermost feelings to strangers who could be predators waiting on the next prey, or children who have no caring ear to listen or shoulder to lean and cry on, or children who are subjected on a daily basis to bullying and psychological torture at the very places supposed to be their safe spaces, all of them need our immediate attention, our time and human resources and our urgent interventions.

The rates of psychosocial dysfunctions in our youth are scary, and if abusive or absent parents could comfortably sleep at night knowing that they did a horrible job adding misery to humanity, I do not think it is right for the rest of us to do the same.

It is a shame when the world is a crowded place but many children feel lonely, and it is a sad reality that many more may sleep with full stomach but their souls sleep hungry or totally empty. It is an extreme form of hypocrisy when many grown-ups put a smiley face everywhere except at their homes and have an energetic and funny interaction style with everyone but are exhausted and depleted of energy and patience when with their own families.

Every moment that passes is now in the past and it will never return, so we have a decision to make and the choice is really ours.

Healthy family dynamics provides the best shield against monsters like ISIS.

Predictions

It is my hope that my predictions are proven wrong, but I expect violent groups to continue to grow, breed and predominate unless we speak up and stand united and shout loudly that we are silent no more, not now and not ever, not when the price is too heavy and not when the consequences are too dire.

GENERATION of ISIS

OMAR REDA MD

Conclusion

Given that they are usually the ones most burnt by its fire, youth need to take an active role in any discussion around extremism and be the driving force towards eradicating that pandemic. The fire of violence cannot and shall not continue to be fueled with the bodies of our youth.

It is through providing a sense of safety, securing basic needs, ensuring that they have a voice, a purpose and feel that they belong, and through empowering the youth with education, employment, building on their high ideals, moral values and expanding their horizons of talent and creativity, that we would be able to help them achieve their full potential and not get tempted by ugly alternatives.

Injustice anywhere is a threat to justice everywhere; we either stand united as brothers or fall divided as fools.

I think that the quote I started this book with, is quite befitting to conclude it.

Frederick Douglass summarized the factors that lead to feelings of unsafety and that make people fear one another:

> *"Where justice is denied, where poverty is enforced, where ignorance prevails, and where one class is made to feel that society is organized in a conspiracy to oppress, rob and degrade them, neither persons nor property will be safe".*

References

The Holy Quran

**Debate on Violent Extremism
United Nations Security Council**
7432nd meeting, April 23, 2015

GENERATION *of* ISIS

Notes

GENERATION of ISIS

Notes

Notes

GENERATION *of* ISIS

NOTES

Notes

GENERATION of ISIS

Notes

الطفولة في زمن داعش

الملاحظات

الطفولة في زمن داعش

الملاحظات

الطفولة في زمن داعش

الملاحظات

الطفولة في زمن داعش

الملاحظات

الطفولة في زمن داعش

الملاحظات

الطفولة في زمن داعش

الملاحظات

المراجع

القرآن الكريم

إجتماع مجلس الأمن بالأمم المتحده حول العنف والتطرّف 23 أبريل 2015

الخلاصه

لأن الشباب هم عادةً أول من يكتوي بنيرانها، فلا بدّ من أن يكون لهم دور نشط فعّال وأساسي في أي حوار حول العنف والتطرّف والإرهاب، ولا بدّ ان يكونوا هم المحرّك الأساسي للقضاء على هذا الوباء العالمي

إن نيران العنف يجب أن تتوقف عن التهام أجساد اولادنا

إنه عن طريق توفير الشعور بالآمان وتلبية الإحتياجات الأساسيه والحقوق المشروعه، وإعطائهم صوتاً وسبباً للحياة والعطاء وشعوراً بالإنتماء، وعن طريق التمكين لهم بالتثقيف والتوظيف والتعليم والبناء بمثلهم العليا ورفع مستوياتهم وسقف توقعاتهم الأخلاقيه والإنسانيه، وعن طريق توسيع آفاقهم والإيمان بقدراتهم ودعم مواهبهم ومساهماتهم، يمكننا أن نرتقي بالشباب الى الغايه التي من أجلها خُلقوا وأن ننأى بهم عن غواية الخيارات القبيحة الأخرى

إنّ الظلم في أي مكان في العالم تهديد للعداله في كل العالم، إما أن نقف متّحدين كإخوه أو نسقط متفرقين كحمقى

إن ألإقتباس الذي بدأت به الكتاب مناسب جدّاً لختمه، فريدريك دوغلاس لخّص أسباب الشعور بعدم الآمان والخوف من الآخر في هذه العباره

متى ما تمّ رفض العداله وفرض الفقر، متى ما إنتشر الجهل وشعرت طائفه معيّنه من المجتمع بأنّ هناك مؤامره منظّمه لاضطهادها وسرقتها وإذلالها، عندها لن يكون هناك أمان لا للبشر ولا للممتلكات

التوقّعات

أرجو من الله أن تخطئ توقّعاتي، لكنَّني أرى أن المجموعات العنيفه ستستمر في النمو والإنتشار ما لم نتوقف عن الصمت ونقف صفّاً واحداً في مجابهتها، لا يمكن غض الطرف وإلتزام الصمت، ليس الآن وليس ابداً، ليس عندما يكون الثمن باهظاً والضريبه عاليه والعواقب وخيمه

الطفولة في زمن داعش

هذه دعوة لأولياء الأمور أن يتداركوا هذا الخطر قبل فوات الأوان فكلّ لحظة تمرّ لا تعود، هذه دعوه للأسره أن تتكاتف وتتعافى لتكون سدًّا منيعاً ضد تيار داعش

الأسره : خط الدفاع الأمامي ضدّ داعش

كطبيب نفساني، يصادفني كثيراً الشعور بالعجب من أنّ أغلب المشاكل التي يتعرّض لها الأطفال والشباب هي للأسف أسريه المنشأ، ولست هنا ألقي باللوم على أحد، أو أقلّل من شأن العوامل الوراثيه او البيئيه في ظهور الأعراض النفسيّه، بل أريد إلقاء الضوء وتسليط الاهتمام على دور الاسره في كسر ظهر الشاب او تقويته

إن الاطفال الذين ينشأون في بيئات محطّمة مليئه بالتعذيب او الإهمال، واولئك الذين تعرضوا للعنف الجسدي أو النفسي أو اللفظي أو الجنسي، وأولئك الذين اضطرتهم الظروف للولوج في دهاليز التعاطي والإدمان والإتجار بالأجساد، وأولئك الذين يلجأون الى وسائل الإتصال الإجتماعي ويحكون عبرها مع مجهولين عن أدق مشاعرهم وأسرارهم وتفاصيل حياتهم، وأولئك الذين لا يجدون أذناً تُصغي او كتفاً يستندون عليها عند الحاجه، وأولئك الذين يتعرضون للعنف والسخريه في بيوتهم ومدارسهم ومساجدهم وشوارعهم، كلهم يحتاجون الى عاجل اهتمامنا وطارئ تدخلاتنا

إنّ معدلات الهشاشه النفسيه في أولادنا مخيفه، اذا كان بعض أولياء الأمور ينامون ليلهم وهم يعلمون أنهم اضافوا للعالم نفوساً منكسرةً وحزينه ومتألّمه فأنا ارى أنه من العيب علينا نحن أن نفعل مثلهم وندسّ رؤوسنا في الرمال

إنه من الخزي أن يكون العالم مكاناً مزدحماً لكن يشعر فيه بعض الأطفال بالوحده، ومن العار أن ينام بعض أولادنا بطونهم ملأى وأرواحهم خاويه وأعينهم دامعه وقلوبهم منكسره. إنّه لشديد النفاق ان يبتسم وليّ الأمر مع الجميع إلا اولاده , وان يكون نشيطاً وذا طاقة وحيويه مع الغرباء ولكن ليس مع أهل بيته.
إن احتياجات أطفالنا النفسيه والمعنويه لا تقلّ اهمية عن حاجاتهم المادّيه

الطفولة في زمن داعش

الحوار بين الحضارات والأديان مهم لمساعدة الشباب على نبذ العنف، لا بد من تعزيز التفاعل الإيجابي بين المجموعات المختلفة الأعراق والتقاليد والثقافات والأديان على أساس من الاحترام المتبادل

لا بد من سدّ الفجوه بين تطلّعات الشخص وواقعه، فالأمل والإيمان من أثمن ما يملك الانسان ومن أعز ما يفقد، اليأس يؤدي بالشخص الى تصرّفات يائسه

من المهم دعم مشاريع طويلة الأجل ومستدامه للشباب وبهم، هم من يقودها ويدفع عجلتها، خصوصاً الشباب الذين يصعب التواصل معهم كالأقليّات وذوي الإحتياجات الخاصه والناجين من الحروب والصدمات وكذلك شرائح المجتمع المهمّشه
.

الطفولة في زمن داعش

يحتاج الشباب الى إعطائهم الفرصه والشعور بالإنتماء وأن لهم أهداف راقيه يسعون لتحقيقها . البعض يقول أن الخطوة الأولى لإنهاء التطرّف هي محاولة فهم أسبابه والعمل على التخلّص من تلكم الأسباب ، وهذا طيف فيه إنهاء الشعور بالمهانه حتى البنيه التحتيه وتوفير العيش المحترم. إن التهميش والنزاعات الطويله وانتهاك حقوق الإنسان وغياب المؤسسات هي عوامل محتمله لانتشار الفساد ومن المهم تناولها بإتّباع نهج شامل

إن تمكين الشباب وحمايتهم من طرق الاستغلال الإلكترونيه الحديثه هو أيضاً أمر مهم كالحد من نبذ الآخر ومن تسهيل التواصل مع وجهات النظر المختلفه حتى لو لم نتفق معها
يجب علينا ان نركّز على أن يشحذ أبناؤنا أسلحة السلام والعداله والتنميه بدلاً من أسلحة الكراهيه والعنف والدمار

يجب ان نثقف ابنائنا في تعاليم الحوار واحترام الآخرين ، تسهيل المناظرات العلنيّه تعطي الشباب مساحة للتعبير عن احباطاتهم قبل أن تتحول الى مشاعر كراهيه ورغبة في الإنتقام . هذا التوظيف القبيح لأبنائنا يمكن مجابهته على نفس المنصّه إن اعطيناهم صوتا وثقة ومساحة حريه واحترام وتمكين

إن الإهتمام بشريحة الأطفال والشباب والنساء من الوسائل شديدة الفعاليه لإحتواء الشباب المضطرب . بعض الخبراء اقترح خطّة من مسارين ، أحدهما عقوبة المخطئ والآخر الصفح عن التائب ، مزيج من اللين والحزم من أجل كسب النفوس ونشر هيبة القانون

تحفيز الشباب على المشاركه في هذه الخطط يحتاج الى خطوات منها تعزيز حقوق الإنسان ، الدعم الإقتصادي ، البُعد السياسي ، الشفاء النفسي والإجتماعي ، بالإضافة الى الجانب الديني والروحاني
إنّ خلق فرص للشباب للمشاركه والشعور بالأمتلاك والإنتماء والتمكين والإحترام ووضعهم في كرسي القياده على المستويات المحلّيّه والدوليّه والعالميّه هي من افضل طرق درء العنف وفض النزاع واستدامة السلام

التدخّلات

يجب أن نحاول الجلوس مع إرهابيي المستقبل ونسمع منهم ونرى الأشياء من منظورهم، من المهم ان نعلن على الملأ أن العنف والإرهاب لا يمكن ارتكابهما تحت اسمنا وديننا، يجب ان نحكي قصّتنا التي تحاول داعش المنحرفة بكل وقاحه تشويهها

كخط الدفاع الأول، من المهم دعم الأُسرة وتقوية دورها لتقود الشباب الى خيارات أكثر أمناً وصحّيّه

محاربة التطرّف تحتاج الى جهود محلّيّه ودعم دولي، طرق التعافي المجتمعيه يجب دعمها فالنفوس الكبار تفكّر في صلاح العالم وتعمل على ذلك بإصلاح أنفسها أوّلاً

التعليم والثقافه من أشدّ أعداء التطرف والغلو، ومن أفضل حلفائنا لتعزيز التسامح والتفّهم، وتقبّل الآخر باحترام تطلّعات وآمال الناس خصوصاً الشباب من أهم الترياق ضد سموم الإرهاب

الحكومات والمؤسسات الأكاديميّه بالإضافه الى منظمات المجتمع المدني والإعلام تلعب دوراً مكمّلاً مهمًّا عن طريق حملات واسعة النطاق لتوعية الشباب المعرّض لهذا الخطر وأسرهم، لزاماً علينا ان نعود بالشباب من خطوط القتال الى صفوف الدراسة وساحات الترفيه

الطفولة في زمن داعش

هذا في رأيي أفضل من الخيار البديل والطريق القصير من الإشارة الى الغير بأصابع الاتّهام واستخدام العزل والتهديد ونزع الإنسانيه من الآخرين واستباحة دمائهم وأموالهم وأعراضهم وأفضل من مصطلح إن لم تكن معي فأنت ضدي، إن لم تكن صديقي فأنت عدوّي

الحقيقه أننا في هذا المركب معاً إما أن ننجوا كلّنا أو نغرق جميعنا، نحن خلفاء الله في أرضه ولن نعمرها بالإقتتال بل بتشبيك الأيادي وتوحيد القوى وضمّ الصفوف باستخدام وسائل التواصل البصري والسمعي واللين والمحبّه والتفاهم والرحمه وطرح البدائل وتمكين الشباب للإرتقاء بهم الى اقصى ملكات ابداعهم

الطفولة في زمن داعش

يحتاج الشباب منّا بدلاً من ذلك الى الجلوس معهم والسماع منهم والتحدّث اليهم وضمّهم الى صدر المجتمع الحنون وتوجيههم، فكل روح تغادر الى الإنحراف هي كمٌّ هائل من الخير وثروه أضعناها بأيدينا وعيبٌ ووصمةً عار على جبين كلٍّ منّا

السبيل لكسب قلوب البشر هي بتمكينهم وجعلهم جزءاً من الحل وليس فقط من المشكله وذلك بأن نستثمر مواهبهم ونصقل إمكانياتهم ونستمع الى همومهم وآرائهم فلا يدرك حرارة النار إلا من اكتوى بها ولا ينبّئك مثل خبير . وهذا يحصل عن طريق مناهج متكامله تهتم بأمانهم الجسدي والنفسي وتوفّر احتياجاتهم الأساسيّه من تمكين وكرامه وحرّيّه وتعليم وفرص عمل وعيش كريم وتعطيهم صوتاً حتى نرى ذلك الوجه الجميل خلف قناع الفقر والتعاسه والألم

عن طريق ربط الشباب بأجهزة صحيه من تعليم وتمكين وسدّ احتياجات يمكننا أن نواجه هذه المشاكل وجهاً لوجه ونستخدم وسائل الوقايه المبكره لتلافي وسائل التدخّل المتأخره، حتى نعبّد لهم الطريق للرجوع الى الغايه التي من أجلها خُلقوا، عبادة الخالق وخدمة المخلوقين وعمارَة الأرض وإستخلافها

البعض قد يلجأ الى العدوانيه عند إحساسه بفقدان الأمان والقدره على التحكّم، ومن هنا تأتي أهمية توفير مساحات آمنه تعطي الشعور بالكرامه والطبيعيه والإتّزان، وتوفّر فرصاً للتعبير الصحّي عن المشاعر، وتتحدى الأفكار المنحرفه، وتعدّل من السلوك غير السوي، وتعزّز من قوة الشخصيه والرضا عن النفس والهويّه، وتجعل الشباب يهتم بعوائله ومحيطه الاجتماعي والديني وينخرط في نشاطات ترفع من كفائته ومحبّته لنفسه وثقته بها عن طريق دعوته لاستثمار مواهبه وامكاناته وتطويرها

البعض قد يرى في هذا الكثير من التعب، لكن صدّقني قارئي الكريم النتيجة تستحق التضحيات، وهذا الطريق الطويل هو الذي تُحمد عقباه وخواتيمه في صحّة واستقرار أبنائنا وجعلهم مسامحين متسامحين قادرين على التعافي وإعادة التأهيل والإندماج وأن يكونوا اعضاء فاعلين ومواطنين صالحين مساهمين في عملية البناء والإصلاح

وسائل الوقايه

الأطفال الأكثر عرضه للعنف والتطرّف يحتاجون اهتمامنا العاجل وعوننا، لا غضبنا وعقوبتنا. يحب ان نصل اليهم اولاً قبل ان يتمادوا في هذا الفج العميق المظلم

من أجل ان نستطيع إبعاد الشباب عن الأفكار المنحرفه العنصريّه والجاهله والمتطرّفه، علينا أولاً أن نفهم أسباب انجذابهم الى هذه المدارس من الأفكار والسلوكيّات. ما هي القوى الدافعه التي تؤدي بشباب صغار السن الى قطع اتّصالاتهم بأهلهم والى هجر شبكات الدعم النفسي والإجتماعي الصحيّه المتوفره لهم عن طريق عوائلهم وأصحابهم ودينهم

لا نستطيع دفع العنف بالعنف فذلك فقط يؤدي الى تأكيد مبدأ العنف في فض النزاعات، الجهل لا يُمحَى إلا بالتثقيف والتوعيه. يجب أن نجلس مع هذه الأرواح الحائره والنفوس المضطربه ونستمع الى قصصهم ونمسح جراحاتهم ونسدّ احتياجاتهم الأساسيّه خصوصاً العاطفيّه

فقط عن طريق اللين والرحمه والحنان وفتح جسور تواصل وثقه يمكن للجراح أن تتعافى وتندمل وتطيب. القضاء على العنف بالقوّة والعقاب ليست إلا اسطوره، فالعنف لا يخلّف إلا مشاعر سلبيّه وأفكار عدوانيّه تؤدي في النهايه الى مزيدٍ من سفك الدماء

النيران التي تذكّيها وسائل الإعلام وتصبّ زيتاً على بنزينها ستؤدي إلى حرائق مدمّره تلتهم كل شيئٍ في طريقها

معاناة الشباب المسلم تحت ظلّ داعش

الشباب المسلم اليوم يعيش معاناةً كبيرة غير عادله في زمن غول داعش، التحريض الإعلامي ضد الإسلام من الساسه ومحبّي الشهره ووسائل الإعلام هي لعبة تسعى لتحقيق مبدأ فرّق تسُد، واللاعبون خلف الكواليس يعلمون جيداً أن الخاسر الأكبر هم عادةَ الشباب الذين قد يضطرون بسبب هذه الضغوط إمّا للشك في هويّتهم وثقافتهم ودينهم، قد يشعرون بالحاجه للإعتذار عن جرائم ليس لهم يدٌ فيها، قد يدفعهم ذلك إما للإنطواء والعزله أو إلى طرف النقيض من ذلك والتعبير بالعنف والهجوم المضاد

الشباب المسلم في الغرب وجد نفسه في وضع صعب للغايه حيث أن كل حركاتهم هي تحت المجهر وهذا لعمري إجهاد نفسيّ غير مُستَحق ولا عادل

ما يؤلم قلبي ويحزّ في خاطري ان الأطفال الذين يعيشون تحت ظلّ هذه الظروف يفقدون الكثير من طفولتهم وفرص التعايش الصحّي مع ثقافات وأديان أخرى. ليس من الضروره أن نكون كالحساء ونذوب في ثقافة الآخر بل كوننا كسلَطه الفواكه جميلة وشهيه بألوانها ومختلف اطعمتها، خصوصيتنا في كوننا مختلفين، التميّز شيئ جيد، كلنا كألوان قوس قزح نضيف جمالاً الى هذه الفسيفساء البشريه والمتّسقة بكوننا نحن

أنماط القابليّه للعنف

أزمة الهويّه
ضغوط نفسيّه، عائليّه، اجتماعيّه، اقتصاديّه، أو اكاديميّه
الشعور بعدم القدرة على تحقيق الذات وبلوغ الأهداف
النشاطات الإجراميه والتعاطي والإدمان

من المهم هنا كون العالم أصبح قريةً صغيره التفريق بين من يتعاطف مع المعاناة الإنسانيه ويسعى لرفع الظلم ورفض العنف وبين من يحرّض على القتل والكراهيه والعنف فالفريقان لا يستويان

في الأغلب الخوض في تجارب الجهل والفقر والإستثناء الإجتماعي قد تدفع بالشباب الى الإيمان بالخيال وتصديق الخرافات مما يسهّل عليهم المشي في دهاليز اليأس والهلاوس والضلالات ووديان الدمار والموت

أن تكون لك نظره غير مرنه أو بدائيه أو أن تنظر للدين والسياسه من منظور منحرف لهو امر خطير، يسهّل عليك أن تنزع سطرا من كتاب او جملة من نص لتصبغ دينًا أو مجموعة كاملة بفرشاةٍ واحده

من المهم ايضاً كما أسلفت ان ننتبه لقصص الصدمة، فمن تعرّض للأذى قد يسهل عليه إيذاء غيره، فالجراح التي تُترك وتُهمل قد تلتهب وتتحول الى غنغرينا يجب استئصالها، والضغط دون تنفيس قد يؤدي الى الانفجار

الطفولة في زمن داعش

هذه القائمة ليست شاملة، فبعض الشباب الذين انخرطوا في هذه التشكيلات المسلّحة يأتون من بيئات وخلفيّات متنوعه وحتى متغايره، لكن العامل الاساسي لأغلب من انضمّ الى داعش وغيرها هو القابليّه لتقبّل العنف والشعور باليأس.

الشباب والقابليّة للعنف

لا عجب في أن يسقط بعض الشباب في شراك الأفكار العنيفة بسبب قابليتهم النفسيّة والعاطفية للإنحراف ، ووحوش داعش وطفيلياته تعرف جيّداً كيف تتغذى على فريستها وكيف تقتنص الفرص

قد يقع الشباب في فخ داعش بطرائق مختلفة ، مع التقدّم التقني هذه الأيام فأغلبهم يلاقون حتفهم في الفضاء الإلكتروني . السرّيّة التي يوفرها الإنترنت تعتبر جذّابه جداً لمحبّي الظلام من أمثال داعش

هناك أسباب عديدة قد تجعل من الطفل او الشاب أكثر عرضةً وقابليّة لتقبل العنف ، منها
تربية أسريّه مفككه ، وهنا يحاول الطفل ملء فجوه عاطفيّه وأن ينتمي الى شبكة دعم وحنان لم تتوفر له في صغره
العزلة والأنطواء
فقد شبكة الدعم والتواصل النفسيّه والإجتماعيّه الصحيّه
التعرّض للعنصرية والتمييز
فقدان الاهداف الأساسيّه والمثل العليا في الحياة
ضغط الأقران

العلامات الدالة ونواقيس الخطر قد تشمل
بعد الشاب عن عائلته ومحيطه الداعم
الشك في الهويه والدين والمعنى من الحياة والانتماء
الإهتمام بأفكار وتصرفات عنيفه أو متطرّفه
التغيّر في صفة الحديث والتصرّف

الطفولة في زمن داعش

خوفي الشديد وإشفاقي على أحداث سن تعرضوا لغسيل ادمغتهم وشراء ذممهم للإنخراط في صفوف جماعات عنيفة متشدّدة، هم يواجهون التعذيب من قبل زعماء هذه العصابات الوضيعه ثم يمرّون بألم تجربة قتل أو إيذاء الغير، والكثير منهم قد لا يرى مخرجاً من هذا النفق المظلم والتجربة المخيفة إلا بالمزيد من العنف أو الإدمان أو حتّى الإنتحار

خوفي الشديد وإشفاقي على أحداث سن تعرضوا لغسيل ادمغتهم وشراء ذممهم للإنخراط في صفوف جماعات عنيفة متشدّدة، هم يواجهون التعذيب من قبل زعماء هذه العصابات الوضيعه ثم يمرّون بألم تجربة قتل أو إيذاء الغير، والكثير منهم قد لا يرى مخرجاً من هذا النفق المظلم والتجربة المخيفة إلا بالمزيد من العنف أو الإدمان أو حتّى الإنتحار

الشباب والعنف

يسبّب العنف شروخاً نفسيّة طويلة الأمد. الأطفال الذين تعرضوا لمشاهد العنف وأسلحة الحروب الكريهة قد يعانون من تبعاتها النفسية لعقود او لأجيال، وهذه ضريبة باهظه لا تقدر البشريّه على دفعها

الحرب والقتل هي حقائق بغيضه حتّى عند الضروره، فنتائجها السلبيّه قد تظل الى الأبد في نفسيّة الناجين منها. والأطفال معرّضون أكثر كونهم يميلون للوم انفسهم فيما تعرّضت له عوائلهم، ولأنّه من أجل ان ينمو الطفل شخصيّة صحيّة متّزنة فلا بد له أن يؤمن أنّ العالم مكان آمن وأنه يستطيع الوثوق بالبالغين لحمايته وتلبية احتياجاته الأساسيّه. الحرب للأسف تحطّم هذه المعاني، فالأطفال الذين شاهدوا مناظر القتل والاغتصاب والتخويف والتعذيب والإذلال والمهانه والاضطهاد قد يعانون من أفكار وتصرّفات ومشاعر سلبيّه تشوّش وتشوّه مستقبلهم وتحيّر أولياء أمورهم، ومن هنا كانت أهميّة التثقيف النفسي. يجب على البالغين إذن أن يكونوا قدوة حتى لا ينشأ الأطفال معتقدين ان العنف وسيله لفضّ النزاعات

إضطراب كرب ما بعد الصدمة ظاهرة شائعة بعد حصول حوادث صادمة وقد تؤدي بالناجي إلى إعادة معايشة التجربة في شكل كوابيس أو تجنب كل شئ يذكر بالصدمة أو حصول اعراض جسديّة كالتعرّق والرعشة وزيادة نبضات القلب، وفي حالة الاطفال قد تظهر عليهم أعراض تؤثر على تعاملاتهم الإجتماعيه أو تصرّفاتهم أو تحصيلهم الاكاديمي

الطفولة في زمن داعش

بإمكان كل شخص اقتباس بعض العبارات من أي نص وتحريفها لتحقيق أغراض شخصيّة. فليس من مصلحة احد منّا توجيه أصابع الإتهام الى الآخر أو الخوف من المجهول، خير علاج للجهل هو التثقيف، فلنطلب المعرفه إذاً ولنحاول إيجاد أجوبة لتساؤلاتنا. إذا مددنا أيدينا وبنينا جسور تواصل وثقة فقد نسعد باكتشاف أن لدينا من النقاط المشتركة أكثر من نقاط الخلاف مع ذلك الآخر

ماذا يقول الاسلام عن داعش

ليس بين الإسلام و داعش اي عوامل مشتركه، بل بالعكس فالإسلام يأمر أتباعه بإنقاذ الأرواح ونشر الفرح والسلام. يعلمنا القرآن الكريم أنّه من قتل نفساً فكأنما قتل الناس جميعاً ومن أحياها فكأنما احيا الناس جميعاً. ويخبرنا رسول الإسلام محمد عليه افضل الصلاة والسلام أن حرمة دم المسلم أشدّ عند الله من حرمة الكعبه

الحرب إذن ليست بين الإسلام والغرب، الحرب التي يجب أن تشتعل هي ضد كل أشكال داعش من جهل وكراهية وعنصريّة؛ حرب سلميّة أسلحتها التوعيه والمحبّة والتواصل ولمّ الشمل

لا يوجد أيّ دين يحض على القتل والعنف، بل الخالق سبحانه يحرّم ويجرّم كل أشكال الإيذاء؛ الجسدي واللفظي والمعنوي والعاطفي. الرّب سبحانه وكل التعاليم السماويه الأصيلة لا تعلم إلا الخير والأمان لكل البشريّة

كنت قد تفحّصت القرآن الكريم وفتّشته آيةً آيه، محاولاً إيجاد أيّ دليل أنّه كتاب شيطاني يحرّض على العنف، ما وجدته إن الله قد أعطانا تعاليم وأوامر ثم ترك لنا حرية الإختيار، فعلينا تقع مسؤولية كيفية التعامل مع ما طلبه منّا وعلينا تقع تبعيّة القرارات التي نتّخذها

لست انفي هنا وجود مجموعات تنتمي لدين الإسلام تحرّف القرآن عن مواضعه لتحقيق أهداف دنيئة كتبرير مشروعية الكراهية والعنف؛ لكن هذه المجموعات المنحرفه تشترك في متشابهات كثيره مع أعداء الدين لا مع اتباعه في تحريف النص المقدّس وخلق الأكاذيب

الطفولة في زمن داعش

داعش ليست فقط ما يسمى بالدولة الإسلامية، بل مصطلح سأستخدمه لوصف ظاهرة ليس لها أية علاقة بدين ولا تعاليم ربّانيه. إنني مؤمن بأنّ ما يسمّى بتنظيم داعش ليس إلا مجموعة من المرتزقة وضعاف النفوس الذين تم شرائهم من قبل النخبه لتحقيق مآرب مفسدة ووقف عجلة الإصلاح حول العالم

داعش لا يمكن دحرها بالصمت عن الظلم أو الاكتفاء بالفرجه على مشاهد العنف. ألانقسام والخوف من الآخر وكراهية بعضنا هو اقصى طموحات داعش والهدف الذي تسعى هذه المجموعة الى تحقيقه

الطفولة في زمن داعش

لقائي الاحدث والأبشع مع الصدمة كان حينما سألتني طفلتي ذات الإثني عشر ربيعاً بابا ما الذي يعنيه ان أرى في الكابوس أنّي أتلقّى تهديداً بالموت، لم أكن اعلم ان طفلةً في ذلك العمر الصغير تستطيع وضع تلك الكلمات الكبيرة والمخيفة في جملة واحدة. حاولت وأمّها ان نحمي بناتنا الثلاث من رسائل الكراهية والتمييز العنصري لكن أولادنا أذكياء ويحسّون مثلنا بالخطر. قرّرت عندها أن أكسر جدار الصمت وأن اقف وجهاً لوجه ضد تيار الخوف والكراهيه. هذا الكتاب هو محاوله متواضعة مني للوقوف في وجه سيل جارف قد يغرقني أو يقتلني ؛ لكنّها مسؤوليتي الأخلاقية وأمانةً تجاه أولادي أن اعمل لجعل مستقبلهم أفضل وعالمهم أجمل ، عالمٌ ملئٌ بالشفاء والمحبة والسلام

يجب أن نعترف بالجراح غير المرئيّة، وأن نكرم قصص الصدمه بالاستماع إليها باهتمام حتى يحصل الشفاء ولو متأخراً وليس ذلك بعيب، بل العيب أن نستمر في الخطأ بعد معرفة الصواب. لقاءاتي المتكررة مع عديد الصدمات والجانب المظلم من الانسانية جعلني أقوى وأعطاني دافعاً لأحمل هذه الرسالة وأمشي فخوراً بقصتي وثقافتي ولهجتي وديني، ولزامٌ عليّ ان اشرككم في هذا العمل لنكون مصابيح أمل وشفاء وأصوات عقل وسلام؛ حتى لا نستسلم لوحش داعش

ليس سرّاً أنّ مجموعات عديده على مرّ التاريخ إدّعت العمل تحت مظلّة الدين من اجل تحقيق أغراض ماديّة ودنيويه قصيرة الأمد. الأيديولوجيات العنيفة ظهرت منذ بدء الخليقة ولا علاقة لها بأيّ دين

ما يسمّى بالحرب على الإرهاب للأسف خلقت سرطاناً خبيثاً للغاية إنتشر بمعدّلٍ مخيف منذ عام 2001. لم يعد بإمكان أحد إدّعاء الشعور بالأمان في ظل هذا العنف والكراهيه. الشر لا يحدث هناك، في مكان آخر بل للأسف أصبح حضوره علنياً ووقحاً في وسط منازلنا وحتى في غرف نومنا. إنها مسؤولية كل واحد منّا أن يعمل ما بوسعه من أجل القضاء على هذا الوحش البشع وإلّا فسنعيش كلّنا تحت ظل حكم جيل غاضب

الطفولة في زمن داعش

جئت الى الولايات المتحدة عام 2002، وتكررت قصّة مأساة الهجرة حيث كانت جراح الحادي عشر من سبتمبر لا زالت طازجةً ونازفة، لكن لماذا عليّ أن اعتذر نيابةً عن جماعةٍ لا تربطني بهم أيّ صلة، ولماذا أدفع أنا واسرتي الضريبة الباهظة للجهل والتمييز العنصري

بدأت الامور بالتحسّن عام 2006 عندما تمّ قبولي لبرنامج الصحّة النفسيّة العالمية عن طريق جامعة هارفارد، تعلّمت خبرات مهمّة جدّدت محبّتي لمجال علاج الصدمة وكيفية التعامل مع الندوب الخفيّة والجروح الغير مرئيّة للحروب والكوارث

عام 2011 دخلت بلدي ليبيا في أتون حرب دمويّة بعد قيام الشعب بثورة اطاحت بدكتاتور ولم تنه عواقبه. خمس سنوات مرت ولا زال الليبيون يقاتلون بعضهم بعضاً، عصابات مسلّحة سوداوية وأفكار منحرفة ملأت الساحة الليبية مهددة بوأد مولود الكرامة والحريّة. هذه الحرب اختطفت اراوح الكثيرين وتهدّد بخلق مجموعات من الشباب تحمل جراحاتها في قلبها مما قد يؤدي الى انتقال الصدمة والعجز عبر الأجيال

قصّة الصدمه صادفتني بقوّة مؤخراً مع إحدى مريضاتي والتي كانت تعاني من هلاوس سمعيّه وتم تشخيصها مسبقاً بمرض انفصام الشخصيّه. عندما جلست معها وسألتها عن الأصوات اخبرتني بأنها تسمع صراخ فتاتين. عندما سألتها عن ماضيها علمت انها فقدت والدها في عمر صغير في حادث سيارة، وقد علمت مؤخراً فقط أن والدها كان في حالة سكر وأنّه صدم سيارة أخرى مما ادى إلى مقتل فتاتين جامعيتين. عندما سألت مريضتي ما الذي فعلته منذ سماعها ذلك الخبر كان ردّها أنّ رسالتها الآن أن تجد عائلتي الفتاتين وتعتذر لهما نيابةً عن والدها. يا له من حمل ثقيل ومسؤولية عظيمة وضعتها هذه الصغيرة على عاتقها ويا لها من مصيبه أن نُضيّع الناجين من الصدمة في دهاليز ومتاهات التشخيصات الخاطئه والأدوية الغير صحيحه ان لم نجلس معهم ونفتح آذاننا وقلوبنا لسماع قصصهم

الخلفية

حدث وواجهت كثيرا من الوحوش البشرية البشعة خلال حياتي بدءاً من عمر ست سنوات حين فقدت اختي ذات الاربعة عشر ربيعاً لسرطان الدماغ. فقدت بصرها اولاً ثم بسرعة تدهورت صحتها رغم محاولات والديّ المستميتة لإنقاذ حياتها. حلمت عندها ان اكون جرّاح مخ وأعصاب، وهذا ما اشعل حماسي لدخول كليّة الطب

اذكر كذلك حينما كاد يتم اختطافي بعمر الحادية عشرة. أوقف سيارته وتظاهر بالسؤال عن الاتّجاه ثم هدّدني إن لم أدخل السيارة، حينها جريت بأسرع ما كنت اتخيّل وراقبته من وراء الأكمه وهو يمشّط المكان قبل أن يفقد الامل وينطلق بسيارته مبتعداً

مرّت الأيام وأصبحت بعمر الثالثة والعشرين طبيب إسعاف وطوارئ، احببت الجانب الإجتماعي والإنساني لمهنة الطب أكثر من الجوانب التقنيّة؛ أحببت الطب النفسي كونه يجمع بين العلم والفن. أعتقد أن السبب الرئيسي لعشقي لهذا المجال هو لقاءاتي المتكررة مع الجراح الخفية والقصص الصادمة

أذكر حين رجعت من المستشفى بسن السادسه والعشرين ووجدت ابي واقفاً بالباب، طلب منّي أن اغادر بلادي على عجل. كون إسمي لسبب او لأخر تم وضعه في القائمة السوداء وهناك أمر صادر باعتقالي اوإغتيالي

هاجرت الى المملكة المتّحدة وعشت حياة طالب اللجوء الصعبة، قابلت أناساً بأقل من عُشر تعليمي ومهاراتي ينظرون اليّ بأزدراء وربّما ظنّوا أنّي هنالك لمنافستهم أو سرقة حقوقهم

المقدمة

للأسف أصبح العنف أحدث الاوبئة البشرية. العالم يصير أكثر خطورة بشكل يومي مع عدم وجود اي علامات لتحسن الوضع في المستقبل المنظور

هذا الكتاب ليس رسالة تشاؤم ولا احباط، بل نظرة واقعية الى الأسباب الجذرية ونواقيس الخطر التي تؤدي بالشباب الى العنف والتطرف، وكذلك محاولة لجذب الاهتمام الى طرق المنع والتدخلات المبكرة قبل تفاقم هذا السرطان القاتل القبيح

السيرة الذاتية للمؤلف

عمر الرضا هو طبيب نفسي حاصل على الزمالة الامريكية ويعيش حاليا مع زوجته وبناته الثلاث في بورتلاند بولاية أوريغون. تخرج من جامعة الطب ببنغازي واشتغل كطبيب طوارئ قبل أن يهاجر الى الولايات المتحدة، تحصل على شهادة ماجستير في الصحة النفسية العالمية من برنامج هارفارد لصدمات اللاجئين، ثم اكمل تخصص الطب النفسي في جامعة ولاية تاناسي

د. الرضا هو مؤسس ورئيس مشروع ليبيا الشفاء ومشروع سوريا الشفاء للتعافى والشفاء وإعادة التأهيل والمصالحة في المجتمعات المتضررة من الحروب، وهو كثير النشاط في مشاريع شفائية عديدة بأمريكا وحول العالم. عمل كمستشار لعديد من المنظمات الدولية ومدرب مع منظمة الصحة العالمية، وكان نائب رئيس الصحة النفسية لدولة ليبيا خلال الحرب

د. الرضا يرأس شعبة إتحاد الاطباء النفسانيين العرب في امريكا، وجمعية الأطباء المسلمين في ولاية ارويغون، وهو مؤسس مشروع الترابط والشفاء للأسرة المسلمة

د. الرضا هو خبير ومحاضر مشهور في مواضيع الصدمة النفسية، الصحة النفسية للمسلمين، الصحة النفسية للمهاجرين، الثورة الليبية والربيع العربي

متى ما تم رفض العدالة وفرض الفقر، متى ما انتشر الجهل وشعرت طائفة معينة من المجتمع بأن هناك مؤامرة منظمة لاضطهادها وسرقتها وإذلالها، عندها لن يكون هناك أمان لا للبشر ولا للممتلكات

فريدريك دوغلاس

سلسلة الترابط الأسري
الجزء الثاني

الطفوله في زمن داعش

النسخه العربيّه

د. عمر الرضا

Family Bonding Project
WORLDWIDE

www.ingramcontent.com/pod-product-compliance
Lightning Source LLC
Chambersburg PA
CBHW020622300426
44113CB00007B/749